THIS BOOK BELONGS TO

In Praise of
HAPPINESS

JARROLD
PUBLISHING

He is happy who knows his good fortune.
  He who is happy is rich enough.
Happiness is the only good.
    The place to be happy is here.
The time to be happy is now.
    The way to be happy is to make others so.

Robert Ingersoll

To be without some of the things you
  want is an indispensable part of happiness.

Bertrand Russell

Joy and grief are woven fine,
  A clothing for the soul divine;
    Under every grief and pine
  Runs a joy with silken twine.

William Blake

IN PRAISE OF HAPPINESS

THE SURPRISE
Vittorio Reggianini 1858–1921

GOING
FOR A PADDLE
Emile Cagniart 1851–1911

IN PRAISE OF HAPPINESS

Joy which we cannot
share with others
is only half enjoyed.
Neither gold nor
grandeur can render
us happy.

Duc de la Rochefoucauld

He is truly happy who
makes others happy.
Those who face that which
is actually before them,
unburdened by the past,
undistracted by the future,
these are those who live,
who make the best use of
their lives, these are those
who have found the secret
of contentment.

Alban Goodier

IN PRAISE OF HAPPINESS

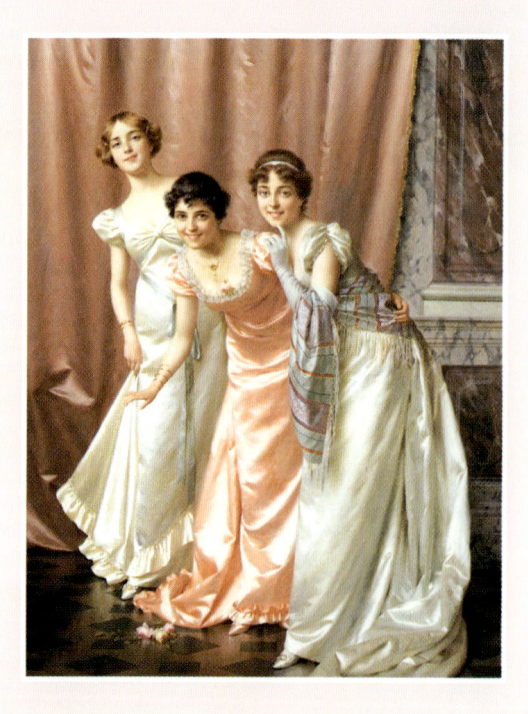

THE THREE GRACES
Vittorio Reggianini b.1858

One joy scatters a hundred griefs.

Chinese proverb

The happy people are those who are producing something; the bored people are those who are consuming much and producing nothing.

Dean Inge

Happiness pursued is like a butterfly always eluding us; but quietly awaited it may alight beside us.

Nathaniel Hawthorne

IN PRAISE OF HAPPINESS

If your joys cannot be long, so neither can your sorrows. The only way to avoid being miserable is not to have enough leisure to wonder whether you're happy or not.

George Bernard Shaw

If you bring sunshine into
the lives of others,
you cannot keep
the rays from yourself.

J. M. Barrie

One is never as unhappy as one thinks,
nor as happy as one hopes.

Duc de la Rochefoucauld

LA RONDE
DES ENFANTS
Gaston de Latouche 1854–1913

IN PRAISE OF HAPPINESS

*H*appiness? – A good cigar, a good meal, and a good woman – or a bad woman. It depends on how much happiness you can handle.

George Burns

Happiness is a mental habit, a mental attitude and if it is not learned and practised in the present, it is never experienced.

Maxwell Maltz

IN PRAISE OF HAPPINESS

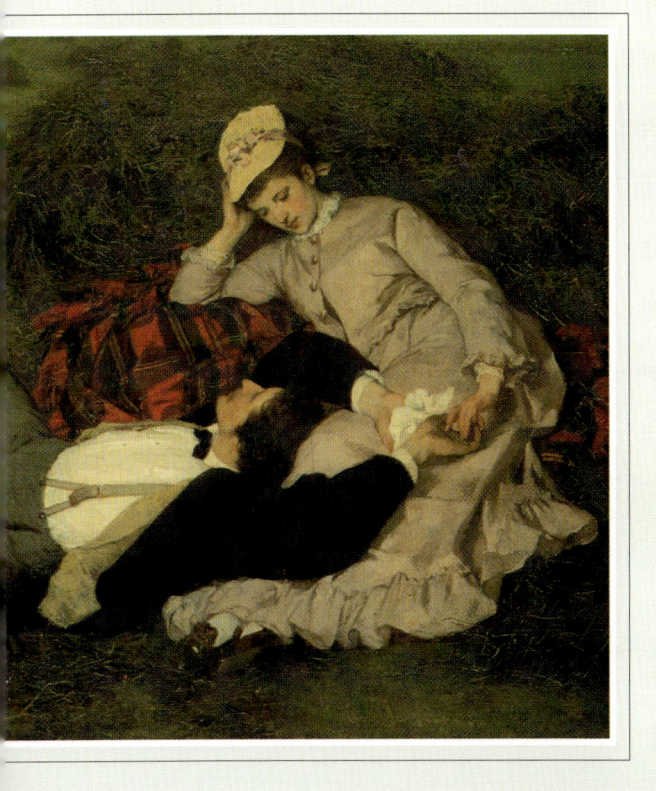

LOVERS
Szinyei Merse Pal

IN PRAISE OF HAPPINESS

SAFE IN HARBOUR
Edwin Thomas Roberts 1840–1917

When a man is happy
he does not hear the clock strike.

German proverb

When one is happy
there is no time to be fatigued,
being happy engrosses the whole attention.

E. F. Benson

When a smile touches our hearts,
when the forest stills us to peace,
when music moves us to rapture,
when we really love, laugh or dance with joy,
we are at one with the angels.

Dorothy Maclean

IN PRAISE OF HAPPINESS

*W*ouldn't life be lots more happy
If we praised the good we see?
For there's such a lot of goodness
In the worst of you and me.
You have to believe in happiness
Or happiness never comes.

Douglas Malloch

Happiness is found in doing,
not merely in possessing.
There is only one
happiness in life,
to love and be loved.

George Sand

A FAMILY SING-SONG
Brita Barnekow b.1868

AN OUTING
IN THE COUNTRY
Marie François Firmin-Girard
1838–1921

All happiness is in the mind. Happy is the man who does all the good he talks of. The truth is, most of us believe in trying to make other people happy only if they can be happy in ways which we can approve.

Robert Lynd

IN PRAISE OF HAPPINESS

A SUMMER'S DAY
Edward Killingworth Johnson
1825–1923

*H*appiness is not a horse;

you cannot harness it.

Russian proverb

The man that is happy in all things
is more rare than the phoenix.

IN PRAISE OF HAPPINESS

THE THREE AGES (*DETAIL*)
Gustav Klimt 1862–1918

Laugh and the world
laughs with you,
weep and you weep alone.
If you cannot have everything,
make the best of everything
you have.

Many persons have a wrong idea
of what constitutes true happiness.
It is not attained through self-
gratification but through fidelity
to a worthy purpose.

Helen Keller

*H*appy is he that is content.

IN PRAISE OF HAPPINESS

BEGGING FOR FAVOURS
Samuel Sidley
1829–1896

If you depend on others to make you happy
you'll be endlessly disappointed.

Most people
are about as happy as
they make up their minds to be.

Abraham Lincoln

It is impossible
to feel angry
if one has a smile
on one's face.

Chinese proverb

People are always happy
where there is love,
because their happiness
is in themselves.

Leo Tolstoy

IN PRAISE OF HAPPINESS

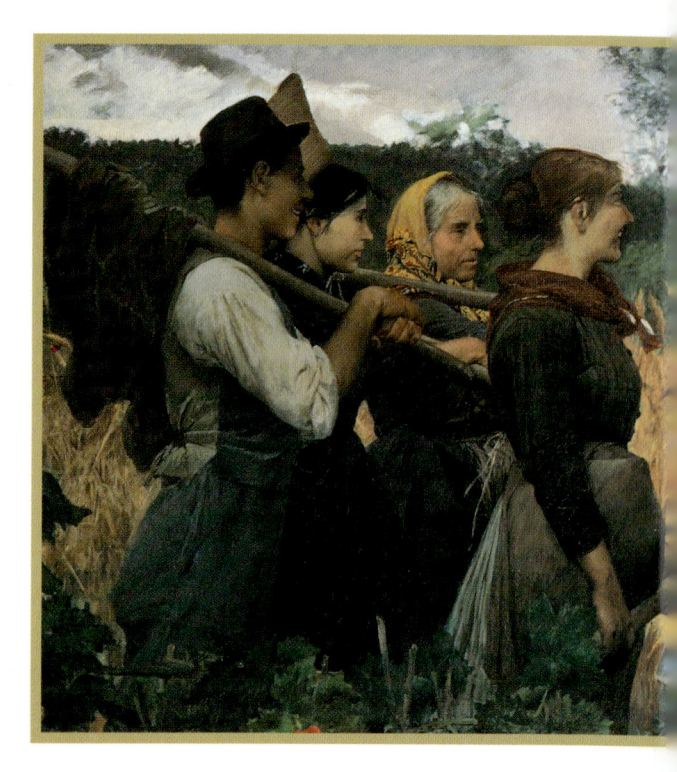

IN THE FIELDS
Egisto Ferroni 1835–1912

About 90% of the things
in our lives are right and
about 10% are wrong.
If you want to be happy
concentrate on the 90%
and ignore the 10%
that are wrong.

Duc de la Rochefoucauld

True happiness is to no place
confined, but still is found in a
contented mind.

To *feel* that one has a *place*
in life solves half the problem
of contentment.

George E. Woodberry

Happiness is like manna,
it is to be gathered and enjoyed every day.

Tryon Edwards

If any man be unhappy,
let him know it is by reason of himself alone.

Dhammapada

True happiness lies not in getting what
you want, but in wanting what you've got.

Giving never
impoverishes.
Withholding never
enriches.

HOOKED!
Edwin Thomas Roberts
1840–1917

· ALSO IN THIS SERIES ·

In Praise of Friends
In Praise of Mothers
In Praise of Children

ALSO AVAILABLE

Cats – In Words and Pictures
Dogs – In Words and Pictures
Golf – In Words and Pictures
Women – In Words and Pictures

First published in Great Britain in 1996 by
JARROLD PUBLISHING LTD
Whitefriars, Norwich NR3 1TR

Developed and produced by
FOUR SEASONS PUBLISHING LTD
1 Durrington Avenue, London SW20 8NT

Text research by *Pauline Barrett*
Designed in association with *The Bridgewater Book Company*
Edited by *David Notley* and *Peter Bridgewater*
Picture research by *Vanessa Fletcher*
Colour reproduction by *Colour Symphony,* Singapore
Printed in Dubai

Copyright © 1996 Four Seasons Publishing Ltd

All rights reserved.

ISBN 0-7117-0863-0

ACKNOWLEDGEMENTS

Four Seasons Publishing Ltd would like to thank all those
who kindly gave permission to reproduce the words and visual
material in this book; copyright holders have been identified
where possible and we apologise for any inadvertent omissions.

We would particularly like to thank the following
for the use of pictures: *Bridgeman Art Library, e.t. archive,
Fine Art Photographic Library.*

Front Cover: DANSE À LA CAMPAGNE, *Pierre-Auguste Renoir* 1841–1919
Title Page: A GARDEN HARVEST, *Frederick Smallfield* 1829–1915
Frontispiece: UNE CHAUMIÈRE ET UN COEUR, *Henri-Gaston Darien* 1854–1913
Back Cover: A SUMMER'S DAY, *Edward Killingworth Johnson* 1825–1923